Beautiful Bible Stories for Children

3

God's Creation

25

Noah's Ark

47

Joseph and His Coat of Many Colors

69

David and Goliath

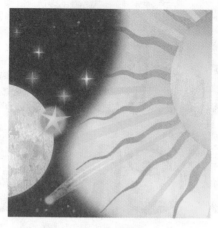

Noah's Ark
Adapted by
Shawn South Aswad

God's Creation, David & Goliath,
and Joseph and His Coat of Many Colors
Adapted by
Tess Fries

Illustrations by
Cheryl Mendenhall

Art direction by
Shannon Osborne Thompson

Edited by
Jan Keeling

First published in the United States in 1998 by Dalmatian Press, U.S.A.

© 1998 Dalmatian Press

Printed and bound in the U.S.A.

The DALMATIAN PRESS name, logos, and spotted design are
trademarks of Dalmatian Press, Franklin, Tennessee 37067.

God's Creation

Long, long ago the world was very different from the way it is now. In fact, there was no world at all! Everything was dark and empty.

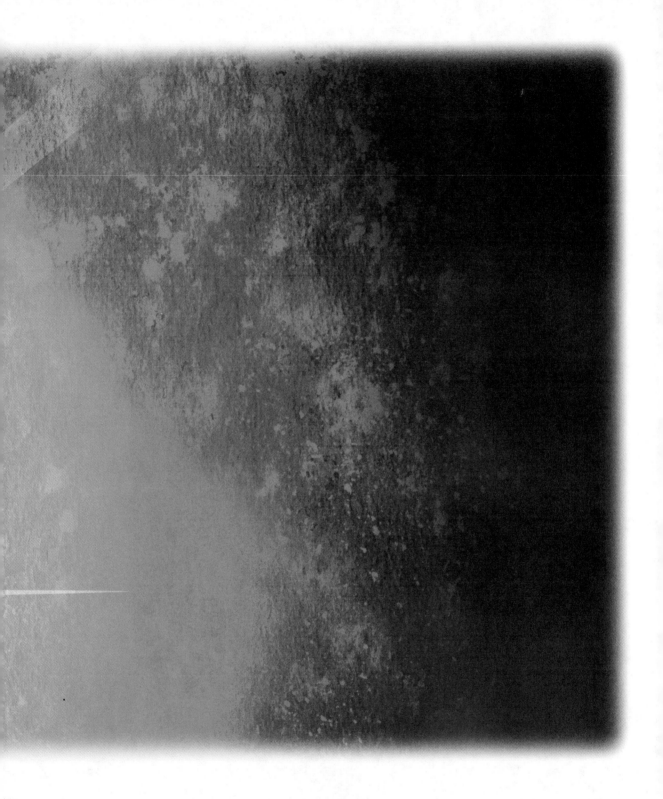

But God was in the darkness, and He had a plan to make something good.

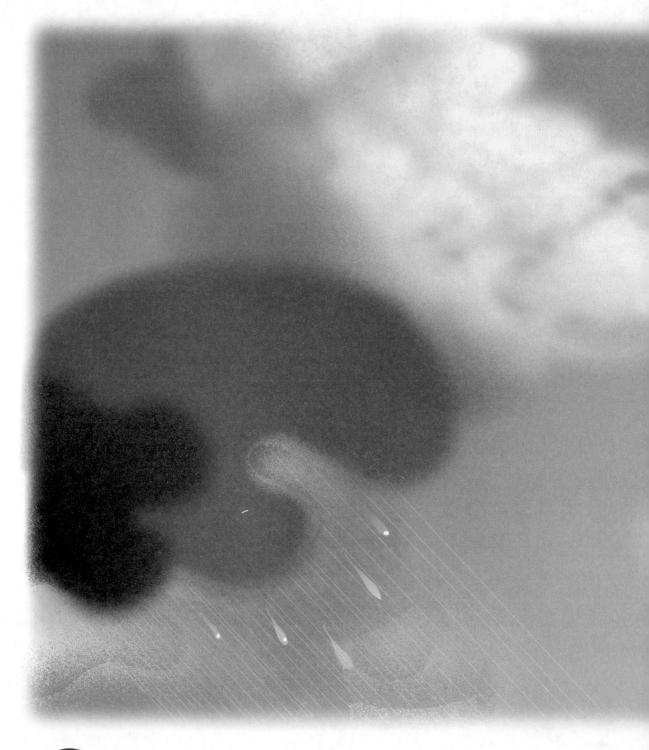

God said, "Let there be light," and a golden light shone
everywhere. He called the light "day" and the dark "night."
This was the very first day.

On the second day, God made the beautiful blue sky. He put the clouds in it to hold the raindrops, and He called the sky "Heaven."

On the third day, God made the sparkling water and formed the seas and rivers.

He shaped the great mountains and the sloping valleys and then sprinkled the deserts with sand.

He planted the fields with tall grasses and trees and colorful flowers. And God saw that it was good.

God put lights in the sky on the fourth day. He made the brilliant sun for the daytime and the gentle light of the moon for the night.

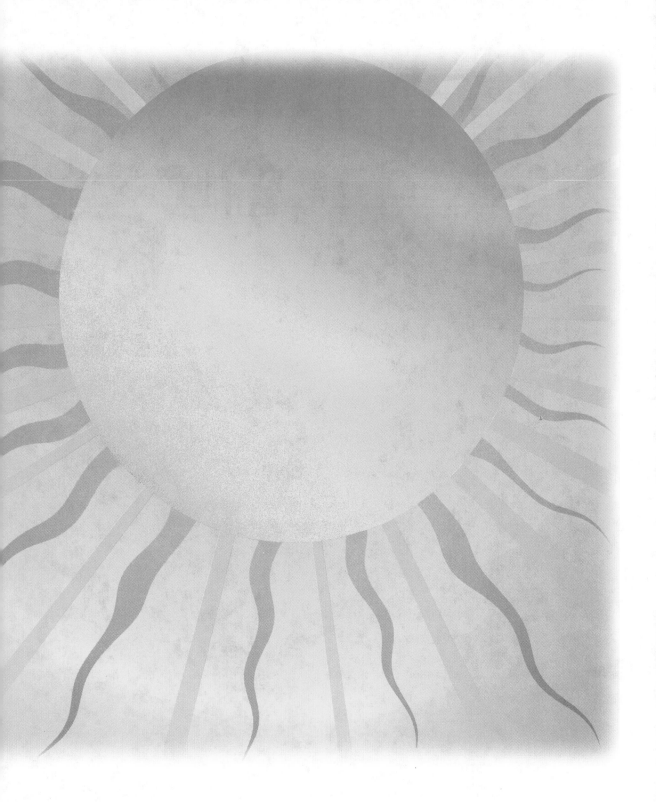

He placed each star in just the right spot and made them all twinkle and shine.

On the fifth day, God made the gigantic whales and the slithering eels. He made the sharks and octopuses and every kind of fish to fill the waters.

God also made the birds to sail on the wind through the sky. He made the mighty eagles, the honking geese, and the tiny hummingbirds.

The next day God made all the animals. He made some with antlers and some with pouches.

He made animals that galloped and animals that hopped...
roaring, growling, and mooing animals.

God wanted someone to rule over the animals, to enjoy His creation, and to love Him. So on the sixth day, God also made the first man.

He made him from the dust of the ground and breathed into him the breath of life. God named the first man "Adam." He named the first woman "Eve."

On the seventh day, God rested, for He was finished.

He saw everything He had made, and He knew that it was good.

God is the maker of all things. There will never be anyone greater or more powerful than He is. God made you just the way you are. He wants you to enjoy His creation and to love Him, for He knows that this is good.

"God saw all that he had made,
and it was very good."
Genesis 1:31
(NIV)

Noah's Ark

Long, long ago there lived a very special man whose name
was Noah. Noah was special because God chose him to do
an important job.

One day God said to Noah, "I am not happy with many of the people and have decided to send a great flood to cover the earth. I want you to build a huge boat. In this boat, I want you to carry your family and two of every other living creature, so that some may be saved."

Noah began to build the large boat, which was called an ark. The ark was strong and sturdy, and it was made of gopher wood. It had one window and one door.

When the ark was finished, Noah gathered together plenty of food. He needed to find enough food to feed his family and all the animals while they lived on the ark, because they would not see land for a long time.

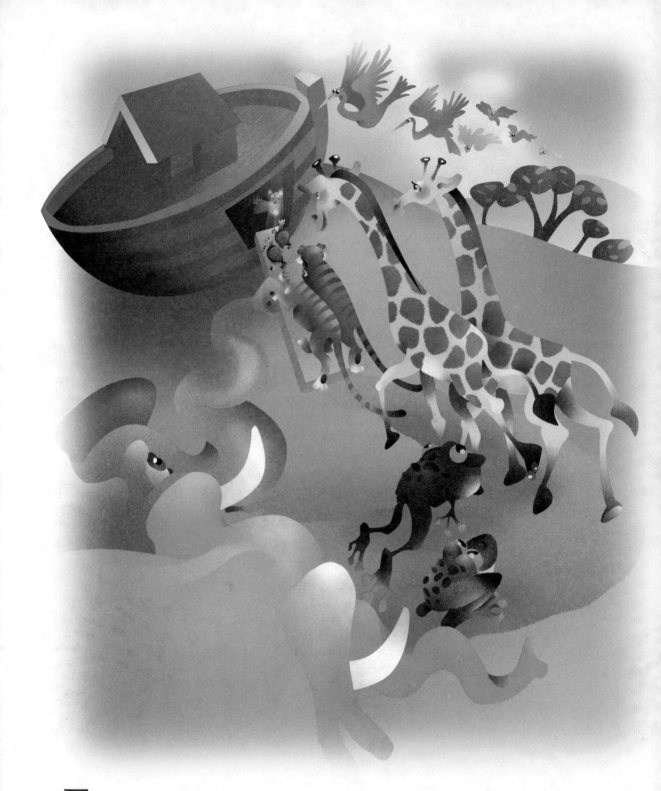

Finally he was ready. Noah's wife and family entered the ark, and then the animals came in two by two. There were animals of every kind. There were two of every bird, every snake, every cat, every horse, and every frog.

Noah had never seen so many animals. The elephants did not look happy. "Don't worry," said Noah, "I have made the ark very large. There is plenty of room for everyone."

The birds fluttered in fear. "Don't worry," said Noah, "I have built the ark very high so you will be able to fly."

The lions roared in anger. "Don't worry," said Noah, "I have gathered lots of food. There will be plenty for everyone to eat."

After every animal was safely on the ark, they heard a loud rumble. It was the sound of thunder … and then the rain began to fall.

The rain poured down for forty days and forty nights. Water covered the earth, and Noah's ark rose high on the water.

After a while the animals became grumpy. The birds were tired of being chased by the lions. The lions were tired of being pecked by the birds. The giraffes were just plain tired. All the animals were bored and ready to run free again.

One day the ark hit something and came to a stop. It made a terrible ruckus. The giraffes fell on the zebras, the zebras fell on the lions, and the lions fell on the frogs. When everyone stood up again, they found they were resting on top of a high mountain.

Noah sent a dove away from the ark to see if the land was dry. When the dove came back, Noah knew the earth was still under water.

Noah sent the dove out a second time, and this time it brought
back an olive leaf. This was a sign that the flood was over.

"Hooray!" cried Noah. "The earth is dry again. We can all get off the ark!" The animals were excited and could hardly wait for Noah to open the door. When the door was opened, the animals rushed outside. The birds flew high in the sky while the snakes slithered low in the fresh grass.

Noah said good-bye to the animals as they paraded off to find new homes. The elephants lumbered over the new land, looking for food. The giraffes glided past in search of tall trees. The frogs hopped playfully towards the ponds. And every other living thing found a new place to live.

Noah and his family were happy with the work they had done for God. God was also very pleased, and He spoke to Noah.

"Noah," said God, "I am very pleased with your work, and I promise never to destroy the earth with water again. Look to the sky between the clouds for a sign of my promise and love."

Noah looked up, and in the sky was the most beautiful thing
he had ever seen. It was a rainbow full of bright colors.

So the next time it rains all day, and you are afraid you will never go outside again, look for a rainbow. It is a sign of hope, and God's promise that the sun will always shine again.

*"I have set my rainbow in the clouds,
and it will be the sign of the covenant
between me and the earth …
Never again will the waters become
a flood to destroy all life."*
Genesis 9:13-15
(NIV)

Joseph
and His Coat of
Many Colors

Once there was an old man named Jacob who had twelve sons. Of all his sons he loved Joseph the most, and he gave him a beautiful coat of bright colors.

Joseph's brothers were very jealous for they knew Joseph was their father's favorite son.

Joseph had two strange dreams about golden sheaves of corn and sparkling stars bowing before him. The dreams meant that one day he would be greater than his brothers.

His brothers were so angry! They couldn't believe that Joseph thought they would ever bow before him.

One day Jacob asked Joseph to go to his brothers who were many miles away taking care of their sheep and cattle. He wanted to know if all was well.

When Joseph's brothers saw him coming they became so angry they wanted to get rid of him.

Reuben, the oldest brother, told them to throw Joseph into a pit. He didn't really want to hurt Joseph and planned to rescue him later. So they tore off his colorful coat and threw him into a deep, dark pit. Joseph begged his brothers to let him out. He was so afraid!

A short time later when Reuben was gone, some traveling merchants came by, and the brothers got another idea. They pulled Joseph from the pit and sold him to the salesmen for twenty pieces of silver.

When they got home, they showed their father Joseph's coat and told him that wild animals had killed Joseph. Jacob cried because he thought Joseph was dead.

The salesmen took Joseph to Egypt. He looked at the towering pyramids and the great Nile River and wondered what would happen to him.

Maybe he thought that God had forgotten about him. But
God was with Joseph.

Joseph was sold to a rich man named Potiphar. Potiphar liked Joseph because he was a hard worker. Joseph was cheerful and always told the truth.

One day Joseph was suddenly thrown into a prison. Potiphar thought Joseph had done something terrible, but he was innocent.

Joseph probably felt all alone in prison, but God was with him.

The butler and the baker for the king of Egypt were in prison with Joseph. One night they each had a scary dream. God helped Joseph tell them what their dreams meant.

Soon the butler went back to work for the King. Two long years later when the King had a strange dream the butler remembered Joseph. He thought Joseph could help the King understand his dream, so the King sent for Joseph.

Again, God helped Joseph and he told the King about his dreams. Joseph said, "God is showing you what He is going to do." He explained to the King that for seven years there will be plenty of food for everyone. After that there will be seven years with so little food that many people will starve. Joseph also told the King how to save food now so there would be enough for everyone later.

The King knew God had made Joseph wise, so he made Joseph ruler over all of Egypt. When Joseph rode through the streets, all the people bowed before him.

Joseph forgave his brothers and invited his family to come live with him.

God did not forget Joseph when he was scared and alone.
He gave him courage and comfort and wisdom. God
knows everything that happens to you, and He will not
forget you either.

*"Now Israel loved Joseph more
than all of his other sons, because
he had been born to him in his
old age; and he made a richly
ornamented robe for him.."*
Genesis 37:3
(NIV)

David and Goliath

Once there was a young shepherd boy named David. David was a happy boy, and he loved God very much.

He wrote and sang many songs that told about God's power and His love for us.

One day, David's father asked him to take some dried corn and ten loaves of bread to his three older brothers who were fighting in the army for King Saul.

David left the next morning. When he got to the army's camp on the mountain, he ran to see his brothers. He was so excited!

But the enemy's camp was right across the valley. As David
ran to his brothers, he saw a giant of a man named Goliath.
Goliath was the biggest man David had ever seen!

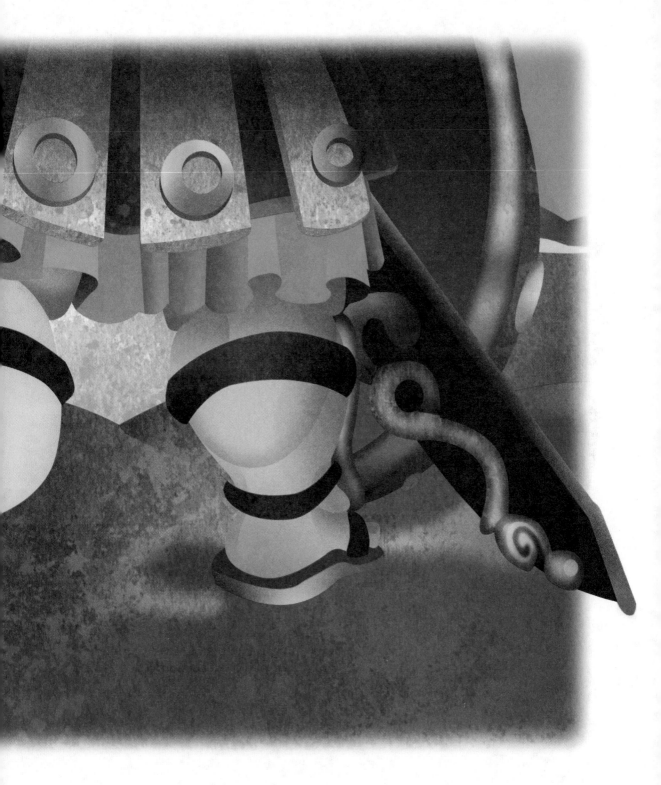

Goliath was covered with shiny armor and carried a huge sword, a shield, and a spear. He stood with his weapons and shouted across the valley.

David's brothers told him that for forty days Goliath had been shouting at them. Every morning and every night he shouted at King Saul's soldiers to send someone out to fight him. Goliath shouted, "If any of you can defeat me, your King's army will be the winner of the whole battle and we will be your servants."

The King's soldiers were so afraid that they ran away when they saw Goliath. But David was not afraid.

David went to the King and told him that he would fight Goliath. King Saul said, "You are much too young to fight this great giant."

But David would not give up. He knew God was greater than any man. He told the King how, with God's help, he had defeated a fierce lion and a hungry bear who stole a lamb from his flock. David was sure that God would help him fight Goliath!

King Saul believed that God would help David as he had
said. King Saul gave David his armor and sword. David put on
the armor and tried the sword, but he was not used to such
heavy things, so he took only his staff and sling and went
down to the river.

There at the river, David found five smooth stones and put them in his shepherd's bag.

Then David walked toward Goliath. Goliath laughed when he saw the small boy coming down the mountain toward him.

Dav10 was not afraid. "God will help me win," he said.
Then he put his hand in his bag and pulled out one stone.

He put the stone in his sling and hurled it toward Goliath.

It hit the giant directly on the forehead, and he fell to the
ground with a thud.

When the enemy soldiers saw that their mighty giant had fallen, they all ran away in fear.

David had won the battle for King Saul because God had helped him!

When you think you are too young and too small to do help someone else, remember how God helped David defeat the Giant. Nothing is ever impossible for God if you only let Him help you!

*"Reaching into his bag and taking out
a stone, he slung it and struck the
Philistine on the forehead."*
1 Samuel 17:49
(NIV)